TRAILBLAZERS of the MODERN WORLD

JOHN F. KENNEDY

By Michael Burgan

WORLD ALMANAC® LIBRARY

Please visit our web site at: www.worldalmanaclibrary.com
For a free color catalog describing World Almanac® Library's list of high-quality books
and multimedia programs, call 1-800-848-2928 (USA) or 1-800-461-9120 (Canada).
World Almanac® Library's Fax: (414) 332-3567.

Library of Congress Cataloging-in-Publication Data

Burgan, Michael.
    John F. Kennedy / by Michael Burgan.
        p. cm. — (Trailblazers of the modern world)
    Includes bibliographical references and index.
    Summary: A biography of the thirty-fifth president of the United States, who served from 1961 until his assassination in 1963.
    ISBN 0-8368-5065-3 (lib. bdg.)
    ISBN 0-8368-5225-7 (softcover)
    1. Kennedy, John F. (John Fitzgerald), 1917-1963—Juvenile literature. 2. Presidents—United States—Biography—Juvenile
literature. [1. Kennedy, John F. (John Fitzgerald), 1917-1963. 2. Presidents.] I. Title. II. Series.
E842.Z9B87 2001
973.922'092—dc21
[B]   2001034178

This North American edition first published in 2001 by
World Almanac® Library
330 West Olive Street, Suite 100
Milwaukee, WI 53212 USA

This U.S. edition © 2001 by World Almanac® Library.

An Editorial Directions book
Editor: Lucia Raatma
Designer and page production: Ox and Company
Photo researcher: Dawn Friedman
Indexer: Timothy Griffin
Proofreader: Neal Durando
World Almanac® Library art direction: Karen Knutson
World Almanac® Library editor: Jacqueline Laks Gorman
World Almanac® Library production: Susan Ashley and Jessica L. Yanke

Photo credits: John Fitzgerald Kennedy Library, cover, 4, 5; John Fitzgerald Kennedy Library/Dick Sears, 6;
Hulton/Archive, 7 top; Hulton/Archive/Popperfoto, 7 bottom; AP/Wide World Photos, 8; John Fitzgerald Kennedy
Library, 9, 10, 11; Hulton/Archive/Hulton Getty, 12; Hulton/Archive/Scott Swanson, 13; John Fitzgerald Kennedy
Library, 14; Hulton/Archive/Popperfoto, 16; John Fitzgerald Kennedy Library, 17 top; Hulton/Archive/Hulton Getty,
17 bottom; Hulton/Archive, 18; John Fitzgerald Kennedy Library/New Bedford Standard-Times, 19; John Fitzgerald
Kennedy Library/Photo Researchers/Mark Shaw, 20 top; AP/Wide World Photos, 20 bottom; John Fitzgerald Kennedy
Library/Look/Harrington, 22; John Fitzgerald Kennedy Library/Benjamin E. Forte, 23 top; John Fitzgerald Kennedy
Library/Bill Bridges, 23 bottom; John Fitzgerald Kennedy Library, 24 top; Hulton/Archive/American Stock, 24 bottom;
Hulton/Archive, 25; Hulton/Archive/Edinger, 26 top; AP/Wide World Photos, 26–27; Corbis, 28; Hulton Archive, 29;
Hulton/Archive/Hulton Getty 30; John Fitzgerald Kennedy Library, 31; Hulton/Archive/Hulton Getty, 32 top, 32
bottom, 34; John Fitzgerald Kennedy Library, 35; Corbis/Bettmann, 36, 37; Hulton/Archive, 38; John Fitzgerald
Kennedy Library, 39 top; Hulton/Archive/Hulton Getty/Vince Finnegan, 39 bottom; AP/Wide World Photos/Boston
Herald, 40; John Fitzgerald Kennedy Library/Cecil W. Stoughton, 41; Hulton/Archive/Hulton Getty, 42, 43.

Printed in the United States of America

1 2 3 4 5 6 7 8 9 05 04 03 02 01

TABLE of CONTENTS

CHAPTER 1   THE YOUNGEST PRESIDENT   4

CHAPTER 2   FAMILY TIES   6

CHAPTER 3   WAR AND CHANGE   12

CHAPTER 4   POLITICAL LIFE   17

CHAPTER 5   RACE FOR THE WHITE HOUSE   22

CHAPTER 6   PRESIDENTIAL ACTIVITIES   28

CHAPTER 7   DEATH OF A PRESIDENT   36

TIMELINE   44

GLOSSARY   45

TO FIND OUT MORE   46

INDEX   47

THE YOUNGEST PRESIDENT

On January 20, 1961, John Fitzgerald Kennedy was sworn in as the thirty-fifth president of the United States. His presidency was historic in many ways. At age forty-three, "JFK," as he was known, was the youngest person ever elected to the presidency. He was also the nation's first Roman Catholic president.

In spite of his young age, Kennedy had already done many significant things. He published a popular book after graduating from college. During World War II (1939–1945), he served in the U.S. Navy and won honors

President John F. Kennedy delivering his inaugural speech in 1961

for his courageous actions. After the war, Kennedy entered politics and began the career that took him to the White House.

BIG IDEAS

As president, Kennedy had many plans for the nation. He called his overall program the New Frontier. Kennedy wanted to improve the U.S. **economy**, he planned to strengthen the military, and he also promised to make the United States a leader in space exploration. The U.S. Congress did not approve all of Kennedy's plans, but the president remained popular with many Americans. He and his wife, Jackie, seemed to give the whole country a new, youthful spirit and the promise of great things to come.

Kennedy was known for his charm, wit, and youthful spirit.

A TRAGIC HERO

On November 22, 1963, Kennedy's policies and plans came to a sudden halt. While visiting Dallas, Texas, Kennedy was shot and killed. The nation wept for a president who died at such an early age. Indeed, his death was an important moment in many people's lives, marking a turning point in United States history. Kennedy became a hero to many Americans, but over the years, others pointed out mistakes he made during his lifetime. However, despite his flaws, John F. Kennedy remains an acclaimed historical figure. His family continues to play a role in U.S. politics, and he will always be remembered for his accomplishments.

CHAPTER 2

FAMILY TIES

The Kennedy clan poses at their Cape Cod, Massachusetts, vacation home. John is kneeling at left.

People who knew Joseph Kennedy were not surprised that one of his sons grew up to become president. Joseph was John Kennedy's father. He expected John and the other Kennedy boys to do well in everything they did. The large Kennedy family enjoyed a powerful role in the politics of their hometown of Boston, Massachusetts.

John Kennedy's ancestors were among the many Irish immigrants who settled in Boston during the 1840s and 1850s. More than 1.5 million Irish immigrants came to the United States at that time, seeking to escape the poverty and **famine** that gripped their homeland. Millions of Irish people died during this time

of hardship. The luckier ones managed to leave Ireland to settle elsewhere, as Kennedy's family did. John's grandfather Pat Kennedy owned a bar in Boston, where he was also a popular political leader in the Irish community. John was connected to politicians through his mother's family too. His mother's father—his other grandfather—was John F. Fitzgerald, sometimes called "Honey Fitz." Fitzgerald was the first American-born member of an Irish family to become mayor of Boston.

In 1914, when Fitzgerald's daughter Rose married Joseph Kennedy, two important Irish-American families were connected. At that time, Joseph Kennedy did not enter politics as his father and father-in-law had done, however. Instead, he turned to banking. His goal, he once said, was to make $1 million before he was thirty-five years old. Kennedy easily reached his goal and became one of the richest men in the United States.

Joseph and Rose Kennedy on their wedding day

John Kennedy at age eight

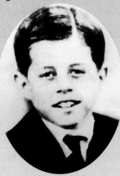

BOYHOOD OF A PRESIDENT

Joseph and Rose Kennedy had nine children. John Fitzgerald Kennedy was their second child and second son. He was born on May 29, 1917, in Brookline, just outside Boston. When John was a young boy, the Kennedy family lived in a wealthy section of New York. John and his brothers and sisters also spent time at the family's homes in Florida and on Cape Cod, in Massachusetts.

At age thirteen, John began attending private schools in Connecticut. At fourteen, he went to Choate Academy in Wallingford. At that time, John was a slender boy, and his classmates sometimes teased him. John was also not the best student. He later said, "I was just a drifter there. I didn't work particularly hard." Despite that, John's classmates at Choate voted him "the most likely to succeed" later in life. John also enjoyed sports, playing football and baseball, racing boats, and swimming.

In 1935, John went to Princeton University because many of his Choate friends were going there. However, he had to leave during his first year because he became sick. Sometimes he was weak and dizzy, and it was years

Joseph Kennedy (center) expected a great deal from his sons Joe (left) and John.

before doctors diagnosed his condition as Addison's disease—a **malfunction** of the **adrenal glands**—and were able to treat him. He spent several months recuperating, and then in 1936, he entered Harvard University. His father had gone to this famous school in Cambridge, just across the Charles River from Boston, and always wanted John to go there as well. John's older brother, Joe Jr., was also a student there.

John Kennedy (back row, third from left) on the Harvard swim team

John and Joe often competed against each other, and Joe usually came out on top. That was one reason why Harvard was not John's first choice of schools. John was always in his brother's shadow. Joe talked about one day becoming president of the United States.

Joseph P. Kennedy

"I wanted power," Joseph Kennedy once said. When he realized that money alone would not give him power, he entered politics. Kennedy encouraged his sons to embrace politics as well. Kennedy made his fortune through investments. He owned a string of movie theaters in Boston. Later, he bought and sold companies that produced films and imported liquor. Kennedy was considered a financial genius, but he could also be mean and would do anything to get his way. He used his money and power to help his family. "The real measure of success," he once said, "is to get a family that does as well as mine."

While John was at Harvard, his father became the U.S. **ambassador** to Great Britain. Joseph Kennedy had become active in national politics. He supported the Democratic Party and President Franklin Roosevelt, and he gave thousands of dollars to Roosevelt's campaigns for the presidency. As ambassador to Great Britain, Kennedy was Roosevelt's "eyes and ears" in a very important country.

During the late 1930s, a major war was about to erupt in Europe. Adolf Hitler, the Nazi dictator of Germany, had built a strong military. He wanted to take over neighboring nations, and he was ready to wage war to achieve his goals. Great Britain and France, with World War I (1914–1918) still fresh in their memory, did not want a second world war in Europe. At first their leaders did not actively oppose Hitler's actions, hoping he would stop short of actual war. Many Americans were alarmed by the events in Europe but did not want the United States to get involved.

John on vacation in Venice, Italy, in 1939

In 1939, John took time off from Harvard to travel through Europe. He wrote letters to his father describing what he saw and heard. By the time John was ready to return home, Hitler had invaded Poland. Great Britain and France now realized they had to fight Hitler to stop his conquests. World War II had begun.

WHY ENGLAND SLEPT

The Book of the Day

Which Explains Why England Failed to Rearm in Face of a Rearming Germany.

In 1938 Winston Churchill re-published, under the title of "While England Slept," the stirring series

Lucid Account of British Policy

WHY ENGLAND SLEPT, By John F. Kennedy. 252 pp. New York: Wilfred Funk, Inc. $2.00.

Reviewed by HARRY L. COLES, JR.

ABOUT TWO YEARS ago Winston Churchill published

Democracy and War Plans

Why England Slept, by John F. Kennedy. New York: Wilfred Funk

THIS SOBER, reliable, straightforward analysis of Great Britain's slowness in rearming to meet the Nazi menace derives additional weight from the fact that the author is the son of the United States Ambassador to Great Britain. He may therefore be presumed to have enjoyed unusual opportunities for first-hand information on the course of international affairs. Its timeliness with problem

BOOKS OF THE TIMES

— By THOMAS C. LINN —

A STUDY of the reasons for Britain's lack of preparedness against German military might ought to interest many people in the United States, especially in Washington, D. C. For, as John F. Kennedy points out in his book "Why England Slept," that country has been the "testing ground" of democratic efforts to cope with totalitarian force. It is from Britain's experience that the United States has to profit if democracy is to be maintained here against totalitarian threats.

"It [England] has been a case of a democratic form of government, with a capitalistic economy, trying to compete with the new totalitarian system, based on an economy of rigid state control. For a country whose government and economic structure is similar to England's and which may some day be similarly in competition with a dictatorship, there should be a valuable lesson."

Since John F. Kennedy is a son of Ambassador Joseph P. Kennedy, this book originated under fortunate auspices. For of all the Americans who have had advantageous positions for studying European affairs in the last few years, those in the American Embassy in London have been among the most favored. Not all young men enjoying such advantages, however, would have shown the will or ability to turn them to such useful literary ends. Young Mr. Kennedy also spent some time in the American Embassy in Paris, studied at the University of London, and is a cum laude graduate in international relations of Harvard University.

This is no time for any one to find fault with individual British statesmen for what they may have contributed to Britain's present plight. Mr. Kennedy is not interested in finding scapegoats but in pointing out for the education of his fellow countrymen the reasons for Britain's tardy rearmament, so that similar mistakes may be avoided here.

This analysis considers the status of armament in England year by year from 1931, when the National Government came into office, to the present time. It traces the gradual change of temper in Britain from pacifism to war.

The basic reason for Britain's delayed rearmament, according to Mr. Kennedy, is inherent in the democratic form of government. Contrasting the weakness of democracy in competing with the totalitarian system, he writes, "Democracy is the superior form of government, because it is based on a respect for man as a reasonable being. For the long run, then, democracy is superior.

"But for the short run, democracy has great weaknesses. When it competes with a system of

"WHY ENGLAND SLEPT. By John F. Kennedy. Foreword by Henry R. Luce. 252 pages. Wilfred Funk, Inc. $2

government which cares nothing for permanency, a system built primarily for war, democracy, which is built primarily for peace, is at a disadvantage. And democracy must recognize its weaknesses; it must learn to safeguard its institutions if it hopes to survive."

In democracies governments dare not act without the consent of the people, and the population of England swung slowly and reluctantly from its desire for disarmament of the Nineteen Twenties to its present war stride. The final and complete awakening to the acute unpreparedness of the empire did not come until after Munich. Only with war at the door did Britain's preparation for war begin with the earnestness which should have marked the effort years before.

For this tardiness Mr. Kennedy believes that no single man or group is to blame. The government, business and labor all had a share of responsibility. The government did not have the vision to foresee the crisis in the offing, business did not want to pay the taxes involved in extensive armament, and labor was loath to relinquish its rights until convinced that war was inevitable.

The tragedy is that England did not begin to rearm in 1934 instead of in 1936. Meantime Germany got a start which Mr. Kennedy believes fundamentally responsible for Munich and England's present difficulties. Munich, he thinks, was inevitable on the basis of British unpreparedness alone, but there was another consideration. "I believe," he writes, "Chamberlain was sincere in thinking that a great step had been taken towards healing one of Europe's fever sores. I believe that English public opinion was not sufficiently aroused to back him in a war."

Armament was retarded by various factors which were peculiar to England. Mr. Kennedy thinks that the country was unfortunate in its choice of men to head the government during this critical period, that there was a lack of progressive younger leadership caused by the loss of a generation in the World War, that the English parliamentary system increased the difficulty of rearmament as did the strong public sentiment in favor of the League of Nations, and as did also "the closeness to the problem of the English aristocracy, which was opposed strongly to war."

It is, of course, too early for any final appraisal of the men and the circumstances that shaped England's policy during the last decade. The information is by no means obtainable yet for such an undertaking. Mr. Kennedy has made a careful analysis from the records that are available. His factual and unemotional approach to the problem is praiseworthy, and his conclusions ought to be weighed carefully in this country. The new publishing firm of Wilfred Funk, Inc. has made an excellent choice for its first book.

Inside Story

John F. Kennedy, son of the United States Ambassador Joseph P. Kennedy, envoy to Great Britain, has written the first publication of the new house of Willard Funk, "Why England Slept."

...war was at its doors until it was almost too late.

While Baldwin and Chamberlain were at fault in failing to give a stronger lead to the national effort and sometimes in issuing soothing statements which were calculated to lull public opinion as to the seriousness of the danger, they had to reckon with the existence of a strong...

brought the empire to the present hazard. But for all that, but for public apathy in the last decade, England would have been so bristling with the defensive and offensive arms of war, and men fit to arm them, that no blitzkrieger would have dared to think of attack.

John F. Kennedy has written in Why England Slept so rational an explanation of national sins of omission as to give a short and direct answer to a question which must have puzzled most of the world. Incidentally, to judge from this first book, John F. Kennedy is a name to watch in the world of books and in world affairs from now on.

During his final year at Harvard, John wrote a paper about Great Britain and the war. After he graduated in May 1940, his father helped get the paper published as a book, called *Why England Slept*. Soon, however, John and other Americans would be doing more than merely reading about war. They would be fighting one.

CHAPTER 3

WAR AND CHANGE

The war in Europe started badly for Great Britain and France. By June 1940, Germany controlled France. The Germans then sent waves of planes to bomb Great Britain. More Americans began to realize that the United States was probably going to enter the war to help Great Britain, a traditional U.S. **ally**.

German troops in Paris, 1940

In the fall of 1941, John F. Kennedy entered the U.S. Navy. John had hurt his back playing college football, but his father used his influence to make sure John was allowed to serve. The young Kennedy was soon assigned to a job in Washington, D.C.

Then, just a few months later, Japan—an ally of Germany in the war—launched a surprise attack on the United States. The Japanese wanted to cripple U.S. military power in the Pacific Ocean. On December 7, 1941, hundreds of Japanese bombers roared through the skies over Pearl Harbor, Hawaii, bombing U.S. Navy ships that were docked there and killing thousands.

The bombing of Pearl Harbor, December 7, 1941

The next day, the United States declared war on Japan, and a few days later on Japan's allies, Germany and Italy, which also declared war on the United States. U.S. troops would soon be fighting on two fronts: Europe and the Pacific Ocean. Kennedy was ready to do his part.

PT 109

John Kennedy was eager to go to sea and help fight the Japanese, and, thanks to his father, he got his wish. Joseph Kennedy once again contacted friends in the U.S. government, who arranged for John to see action during the war.

Kennedy earned the rank of second lieutenant and began training to command a motor torpedo (PT) boat. These small PT boats could move easily through shallow waters and sail on the ocean too. They carried torpedoes to attack enemy ships.

In April 1943, Kennedy took command of *PT 109.* The boat, with a crew of twelve, worked in the South Pacific Ocean. The Japanese had captured many small islands in that part of the Pacific, and now U.S. forces were trying to drive the Japanese off the islands.

Second lieutenant John F. Kennedy

Before dawn on August 2, 1943, Kennedy and his crew were in the Solomon Islands with a fleet of PT boats trying to attack Japanese ships. One of the Japanese vessels cut through the water toward Kennedy's boat and plowed through the right rear end of *PT 109*. The collision killed two sailors immediately. The survivors tried to stay away from the blazing fuel oil on the ocean's surface.

During the collision, Kennedy was in the front part of the boat, which stayed afloat in the water. Kennedy called out into the early-morning darkness, searching for survivors, and his men shouted back. Several were injured, so Kennedy dived into the water and helped them reach the floating wreck of the boat.

The sailors huddled on the remains of *PT 109*, waiting to be rescued, but no ships arrived to help them. Finally, Kennedy ordered the men to swim to an island about 3 miles (5 kilometers) away. Kennedy towed one wounded sailor by tugging a strap attached to the man's life jacket.

Several days passed before the sailors got help from some native people on a nearby island. All the survivors were eventually rescued, and Kennedy was hailed as a hero. He received several medals and was praised by the Navy for "his courage, endurance, and excellent leadership."

Hero of *PT 109*

What follows is part of an official U.S. Navy report on John Kennedy's actions on the morning of August 2, 1943:

*Lt. Kennedy ordered all hands to abandon ship when it appeared the fire would spread to it. All soon crawled back aboard when this danger passed. . . . Lt. Kennedy had to tow [Pat] McMahon, who was helpless because of serious burns, back to the boat. A strong current **impeded** their progress, and it took about an hour to get McMahon aboard PT 109. Kennedy then returned for the other two men, one of whom was suffering from minor burns. He traded his life belt to [Charles] Harris, who was uninjured, in return for Harris's waterlogged kapok life jacket which was impeding the latter's swimming. Together they towed [Ray Lee] Starkey to the PT.*

Joe Kennedy lost his life as a Navy pilot in World War II.

A few months after his rescue, Kennedy left the Pacific. His back injury was now worse than ever, and he needed surgery. He also contracted malaria, a serious disease that is common in warm climates. By spring 1944, he was back in Massachusetts. Shortly thereafter, the Kennedy family received the tragic news that Joe Jr., the family's oldest son, had been killed while serving as a pilot in Europe. The Kennedy family was devastated by this loss.

Joe's death meant that John was now the oldest Kennedy son, and his father expected John to do the great things everyone assumed Joe Jr. would have done. "My father wanted his eldest son in politics," John Kennedy later said. "He demanded it." Soon John would take on the tasks his father had counted on Joe Jr. to do.

JFK's Thoughts on War

After his heroics as captain of *PT 109,* Kennedy wrote a letter to a friend back in the United States. Here is part of that letter:

I received a letter today from the wife of my engineer, who was so badly burnt that his face and hands and arms were just flesh. . . . He couldn't swim, and I was able to help him, and his wife thanked me, and in her letter she said, "I suppose to you it was part of your job, but Mr. McMahon was part of my life and if he had died I don't think I would have wanted to go on living." . . . There are so many McMahons that don't come through.

CHAPTER 4

At the end of World War II, Kennedy briefly worked as a journalist. In 1945, he traveled to San Francisco to report on the founding of the **United Nations**. The next year, John returned to Massachusetts to enter politics, running for U.S. Congress as a Democrat. Still just in his late twenties, Kennedy won a seat representing a part of Boston and surrounding towns.

After the war, John Kennedy was thrust into the world of politics.

IN OFFICE

In Congress, Kennedy usually supported Harry Truman, the Democratic president. Among other things, the president wanted to spend money to build housing for the poor. Kennedy agreed with this and other domestic policies that helped the poor. But Kennedy did not agree with some of Truman's foreign policies.

Kennedy strongly opposed **communism**, the type of government in the former **Soviet Union**. Under communism, the government, led by one political party, owns

President Harry Truman

opposite: John Kennedy and Jacqueline Lee Bouvier were married in 1953.

Senator John F. Kennedy in his office

everything and controls the economy. People living under communist governments do not have the freedoms found in the United States. After World War II ended in 1945, the Soviet Union wanted to spread communism throughout the world—an idea that the United States opposed. The conflict between the two countries was called the **Cold War**, and Kennedy sometimes opposed Truman's handling of the Cold War.

SENATOR KENNEDY

In 1952, Joseph Kennedy wanted John to run for the U.S. Senate. John's brother Bobby managed the campaign, and other members of the Kennedy family donated money. Kennedy won the election by about seventy thousand votes.

Soon after entering the Senate, Kennedy married Jacqueline Lee Bouvier, a beautiful and intelligent young woman. They bought a house in Virginia as Kennedy settled into his new job. He served on committees that dealt with labor issues and how the government was run. By 1956, some Democratic Party leaders thought Kennedy would make a good candidate for vice president.

Jacqueline Bouvier Kennedy

Gifted and attractive, Jacqueline Kennedy became as popular as her husband. Born on July 28, 1929, in Southampton, New York, Jacqueline Lee Bouvier came from a wealthy Catholic family. She first met John Kennedy in 1951, while he was serving as a congressman. Jacqueline worked as a reporter before her marriage.

Jacqueline saw herself as a private person, and becoming a member of one of America's best-known and most powerful families was a great adjustment for her. As First Lady, Jacqueline was always well dressed, and many women copied her fashion styles.

A few years after her husband was killed, Jacqueline Kennedy remarried. Her new husband was a Greek billionaire named Aristotle Onassis. Some newspapers then began calling Jacqueline "Jackie O." She remained a popular figure in the United States until her death in 1994.

LOOKING TOWARD THE WHITE HOUSE

The Democrats had lost the presidency in 1952 when Republican Dwight Eisenhower, a popular general during World War II, beat Adlai Stevenson of Illinois. In 1956, Eisenhower faced Stevenson again. The Democrats who liked and supported Kennedy thought he would help Stevenson win votes among Catholic voters.

In August 1956, the Democrats held a convention in Chicago. Normally, the presidential candidate decides who the candidate for vice president will be. This time, though, Stevenson decided to let the Democrats at the convention pick his running mate. Kennedy was one of several men interested in the position. In the end, however, Senator Estes Kefauver of Tennessee won the vote. Kennedy was disappointed, but not crushed. He called his father and said, "We did our best, Dad. I had fun and I didn't make a fool of myself."

Even more important, Kennedy had shown he was a rising young star in the Democratic Party. American voters would not forget the handsome, charming senator from Massachusetts. After 1956, John Kennedy kept himself in the public eye. His second book, *Profiles in Courage*, won an important award, the Pulitzer Prize, and in 1957 he was named to the influential Senate Foreign Relations Committee. Kennedy now often spoke out about U.S. policies toward foreign countries—especially the Soviet Union.

Profiles in Courage

Profiles in Courage describes the careers of some of the most famous members of the U.S. Senate. At the beginning of the book, John Kennedy wrote about the need for courage in politics:

Today the challenge of political courage looms larger than ever before. . . . Our political life is becoming so expensive, so mechanized and so dominated by professional politicians . . . that the idealist who dreams of independent statesmanship is rudely awakened by the necessities of election and accomplishment. . . . Only the very courageous will be able to keep alive the spirit of individualism and dissent which gave birth to this nation. . . .

opposite: Democratic presidential candidate Adlai Stevenson (right) with his running mate, Estes Kefauver, in 1956

CHAPTER 5

RACE FOR THE WHITE HOUSE

A quiet moment with daughter, Caroline

In 1958, Kennedy ran for reelection as senator. He won easily, and magazines and newspapers wrote about Kennedy and his growing influence in the Democratic Party. Reporters also mentioned his beautiful wife, Jacqueline, who was now a mother, having given birth to their daughter, Caroline, in November 1957.

Kennedy was already hoping to become the Democratic candidate for president in 1960. He had many advantages heading into the race, including his father's money and influence and his own popularity with many Democrats. Still, he faced some major problems.

WORRIES ABOUT HEALTH AND RELIGION

Kennedy's health was still not good. In 1947, doctors had discovered that he had Addison's disease, an illness that makes a person weak and likely to catch other diseases. Kennedy took medicine to control this ailment. His back still gave him great pain too. In fact, until he had back surgery in 1955, he sometimes needed crutches to walk.

Another problem was Kennedy's religion. Throughout the country's history, most U.S. political leaders have been

Protestants, although the **Roman Catholic Church** is the single largest religious group in the United States. Many Protestants would not vote for a Catholic for president. They feared that Catholics were more loyal to the leader of their church—the pope—than to the United States and its laws.

Before Kennedy, only one Catholic—Governor Al Smith of New York in 1928—had run for president, and he had lost badly. Kennedy had to face the prejudice that some Americans still had against Catholics. He tried to convince people that he would not take orders from the pope or any other church leader. "I do not speak for my church on public matters," he said, "and the church does not speak for me." Still, many people doubted that Americans would elect a Catholic as president. Kennedy, however, was determined to try.

Kennedy announcing his candidacy for president, January 1960

Addressing the delegates at the Democratic National Convention in 1960

PRESIDENTIAL CAMPAIGN

Some Democrats did not want Kennedy to run for president. They thought he was too young and needed more experience. Harry Truman said to Kennedy, "Senator, are you certain that you are quite ready for the country? Are you certain the country is ready for you?" Other Democrats thought Kennedy was not a serious politician. When he first entered Congress, Kennedy had not always worked hard. Over the years, however, he had put more effort into his career. Now, Kennedy felt he had the energy and ideas to win.

Kennedy chose Lyndon Johnson (right) to be his running mate.

Richard Nixon was the Republican presidential candidate in 1960.

Starting early in 1960, the Democratic Party held elections called **primaries**, in which Democrats in some states picked the person they thought would be the best candidate for president. Kennedy won several of these primaries and soon became the man to beat. In July, the Democrats held their convention in Los Angeles. On the first vote, Kennedy was named the presidential candidate, and he chose Senator Lyndon Johnson of Texas as his running mate. In his speech at the convention, Kennedy talked about using new ideas and attitudes to make the United States stronger. "For the world is changing," he said. "The old era is ending. The old ways will not do." Kennedy called his plans the New Frontier.

At its convention, the Republican Party chose as its presidential candidate Richard Nixon, who had served eight years as vice president under President Dwight Eisenhower. Nixon had first become famous during the late 1940s as a strong anti-Communist. As president he planned to continue many of the policies started by Eisenhower.

In September 1960, Kennedy and Nixon held the first of four debates. Kennedy discussed how important it was for the U.S. government to help its citizens. He said, "I want the individuals to meet their responsibilities and I want the states to meet their responsibilities. But I think there is also a national responsibility."

The Kennedy-Nixon Debates

The "Great Debates" between John F. Kennedy and Richard Nixon made history. Never before had presidential candidates faced each other on television. Almost 100 million Americans watched the debates. For many people, this was their first chance to see and hear Kennedy.

In the first debate, Nixon chose not to wear makeup. As a result, on television, his face looked pale, even sickly. The television cameras sometimes showed him sweating. Most people thought Kennedy, who seemed handsome and energetic, looked and sounded better than Nixon. The debates may have helped Kennedy win the election.

The presidential debates were not held again until 1976. Since then, all the major candidates have faced each other on television.

THE NEW PRESIDENT

On Election Day 1960, Kennedy cast his vote in Boston and then flew to the family home on Cape Cod. Results came in slowly from around the country. The race was close. Kennedy easily won what is called the popular vote—the votes actually cast by the people—in some states, but lost in others. In the end, Kennedy beat Nixon by just 112,000 votes in one of the closest presidential races of the twentieth century. Kennedy easily won what is called the **electoral vote**, however. Special electors in each state cast electoral votes.

The next morning, Kennedy spoke to some neighbors outside his home. He told them, "I am promising you one thousand days of exciting presidential leadership." Just

a few weeks later, Kennedy had some excitement of his own, as Jacqueline gave birth to the couple's second child—John Jr.

In the months that followed, Kennedy selected people to work with him in the government. He named his brother Bobby as attorney general. In this position, Bobby would serve as the top lawyer for the country. John would also rely on him for advice on many issues.

On January 20, 1961, Kennedy was inaugurated—officially sworn in—as the

The young president enjoyed spending time with his son, John Kennedy Jr.

Kennedy appointed his brother Bobby (right) as attorney general.

president of the United States. On that cold and windy day in Washington, D.C., he gave a speech that outlined what he hoped to do as president. This inaugural speech inspired many of the Americans who heard it. Kennedy was ready to put his New Frontier into action.

Kennedy's Inaugural Speech

Here is part of President Kennedy's speech at his **inauguration**:

Let the word go forth from this time and place, to friend and foe alike, that the torch has been passed to a new generation of Americans—born in this century, tempered by war, disciplined by a hard and bitter peace, proud of our ancient heritage....

The energy, the faith, the devotion which we bring to this endeavor will light our country and all who serve it—and the glow from that fire can truly light the world.

And so, my fellow Americans: ask not what your country can do for you—ask what you can do for your country.

CHAPTER 6

PRESIDENTIAL ACTIVITIES

As president, Kennedy had many plans for the United States. The country was then in the middle of a recession, a time when the economy does not grow. Many Americans were out of work and struggling to pay for food and housing. Kennedy proposed spending more money to help these people. He also wanted to help industries build new factories or improve old ones.

Another important issue of the day was **civil rights**. African-Americans had not always received the same

A civil rights protest in 1960

legal rights as whites, especially in southern states. Starting in the 1950s, many African-American leaders protested this unfair treatment. Kennedy had not always been a vocal supporter of civil rights. As president, though, he began to push for laws that helped African-Americans. Congress, however, did not always give Kennedy what he wanted on this issue and others. The issue of civil rights was tearing the nation apart, and it remained controversial for many years to come. Kennedy encountered opposition to civil rights laws from Republicans as well as from conservative Democrats. Members of Congress also fought the president on lowering taxes.

RELATIONS WITH THE WORLD

The Peace Corps sent volunteers to work in poor countries all over the world.

Kennedy also wanted to help people in foreign countries. In March 1961, he outlined a new program, which he called the Alliance for Progress, to send aid to countries in Central and South America. That month, Kennedy also created the Peace Corps. This new government agency trained Americans who volunteered to work in poor countries around the world. Many young people eagerly joined the Peace Corps.

Kennedy wanted to help other countries while also preparing the United

States for any future war. He thus asked Congress to spend more money on weapons. These included missiles carrying nuclear warheads that could reach the Soviet Union.

Nuclear warheads use power from **radioactive** materials for their huge explosive force. Radioactive materials release radiation, a form of energy found throughout the universe. In small doses, radiation is not harmful, but an exploding nuclear warhead releases deadly levels of radiation. At this time, the United States and the Soviet Union were in a race to build more and bigger nuclear weapons. Kennedy talked tough with the Soviets: "If aggression should come, our response will be swift and effective."

The two countries were also in a race to explore space. In 1957, the Soviet Union launched the first spacecraft. President Kennedy wanted the United States to catch up with the Soviet efforts and take the lead in the "space race." Kennedy said in May 1961, "This nation should commit itself to achieving the goal, before this decade is out, of landing a man on the moon and safely returning him to the Earth."

CRISIS IN CUBA

The conflict with the Soviet Union and communism was now close to U.S. shores. In 1959, rebels led by Fidel Castro took over Cuba—an island just 90 miles (145 km) southeast of Florida. Previously, Cuba had been run by a dictator who was friendly with the United States, and American companies controlled Cuba's economy. Castro took over some of these businesses and promised to improve the government. The United States did not support this revolution, so Castro began to rule as a communist and turned to the Soviet Union for help.

Cuban leader Fidel Castro

Kennedy, like President Eisenhower before him, feared the presence of a communist country so close to the United States. In April 1961, Kennedy approved a plan that had been drafted while Eisenhower was president, under which anti-communist Cubans were trained by the United States to attack the island. The assault came at a place called the Bay of Pigs. Castro's forces easily defeated the attackers, and Fidel Castro now realized that Kennedy wanted to remove him from power.

A large crowd listening to Kennedy's famous speech in Berlin

A DIVIDED BERLIN

Just a few months later, trouble erupted in the East German city of Berlin. After World War II, Germany had been divided into two parts. The United States, Great Britain, and France controlled the western half, while the Soviets controlled the eastern half. The areas controlled by the United States and its allies were democratic, and the Soviet area was under a communist government.

The city of Berlin was also divided in this way. West Berliners enjoyed freedom, while East Berliners lived under communism. Located deep within East Germany, the city presented a special problem for the United States. U.S. planes and trucks had to

A section of the Berlin Wall

President Kennedy meeting with Soviet leader Nikita Khrushchev

follow special routes to bring supplies to West Berlin. Kennedy told Soviet leader Nikita Khrushchev that the United States would never let these routes be closed.

Berlin was also a problem for East German leaders. Normally, East Germans were not allowed to leave their country. Yet they could move freely into West Berlin and go to West Germany or other countries from there. Many people fled East Germany this way, seeking freedom. In August 1961, East Germany began building a wall between East and West Berlin. East Berliners who tried to cross the wall into the West were shot.

After the building of the Berlin Wall, tensions grew between the United States and the Soviet Union. Soviet tanks were stationed in East Berlin. In October 1961, these tanks faced U.S. tanks that had been sent to West Berlin. Neither side fired shots, but both Kennedy and Khrushchev realized they could not risk a war over Berlin. Any actual combat between the United States and the Soviet Union could have led to a nuclear war, which would have killed millions of people.

JFK in Berlin

In 1963, President Kennedy traveled to West Berlin and saw for himself the wall that divided the city. In one of his most famous speeches, Kennedy told the West Berliners that the United States would always protect them. Here is part of that speech:

Freedom is indivisible, and when one man is enslaved, all are not free. When all are free, then we can look forward to that day when this city will be joined as one.... All free men, wherever they may live, are citizens of Berlin, and, therefore, as a free man, I take pride in the words "Ich bin ein Berliner" [I am a Berliner].

MORE TROUBLE IN CUBA

Less than a year after the Berlin Wall was constructed, the United States had another conflict with the Soviet Union. During the summer of 1962, the Soviets began secretly moving nuclear weapons into Cuba. Khrushchev wanted to help defend Cuba from any possible U.S. attack. He also wanted to match the nuclear power of the United States. The Americans had placed missiles in Turkey, which borders the Soviet Union.

When U.S. spy planes reported the Soviet missiles being set up in Cuba on October 22, Kennedy demanded that Khrushchev remove the missiles. The president also said U.S. warships would search all cargo ships heading for Cuba. If these ships carried weapons, they would be turned back. Khrushchev refused to remove the missiles from Cuba. He also said Soviet submarines would attack U.S. ships if they stopped Soviet vessels.

A group of Cuban soldiers preparing to fight a U.S. invasion

Kennedy, determined to get the missiles out of Cuba, prepared an invasion force to attack the island. For the next few days, people around the world feared the start of a nuclear war. Tensions grew on October 27 when Soviet forces in Cuba shot down a U.S. spy plane. Castro said that if a war started, "we will disappear from the map."

Kennedy and Khrushchev finally found a way to end the crisis. The United States promised not to attack Cuba and also to remove its missiles from Turkey. In return, Khrushchev agreed to take his missiles out of Cuba. To many Americans, Kennedy seemed like a strong leader who had handled the crisis well. He had forced the Soviet Union to remove a dangerous threat close to U.S. shores.

Kennedy Speaks on the Cuban Missile Crisis

On October 22, 1962, President Kennedy appeared on television to tell Americans about the Soviet missiles in Cuba. Here is some of that speech:

Within the past week unmistakable evidence has established . . . that a series of offensive missile sites is now in preparation on [Cuba]. The purposes of these bases can be none other than to provide a nuclear strike capability against the Western Hemisphere. . . .

Our unswerving objective . . . must be to prevent the use of these missiles against this or any other country and to secure their withdrawal or elimination from the Western Hemisphere...

My fellow citizens, let no one doubt that this is a difficult and dangerous effort on which we have set out. . . . Many months of sacrifice and self-discipline lie ahead—months in which both our patience and our will may be tested, months in which many threats and denunciations will keep us aware of our dangers. But the greatest danger of all would be to do nothing.

CHAPTER 7

DEATH OF A PRESIDENT

The presidential motor-cade in Dallas, Texas, on November 22, 1963

Pᴿresident Kennedy's car rolled through the streets of Dallas, Texas. As thousands of people cheered, the president waved from the back of his convertible with Jacqueline at his side. It was November 22, 1963, and Kennedy had come to Texas to speak at the opening of a military hospital. He was also hoping to attract voters for the 1964 presidential election.

Kennedy planned to go to Austin, Texas, next. Part of his speech there was going to be about civil rights. Kennedy was trying to do more to make sure African-Americans received fair legal treatment. Earlier in the year, the Reverend Martin Luther King Jr. had been arrested in Birmingham, Alabama. King was a leader of the civil rights movement, and he had gone to Birmingham to protest the treatment of blacks there. Kennedy took steps to make sure King was not harmed while he was in jail. Kennedy also kept working for new laws to guarantee civil rights.

Martin Luther King Jr. received support from President Kennedy.

Kennedy wanted to tell his supporters in Austin, "We have, in the past three years . . . opened more new doors to members of minority groups . . . than had been opened in any three-year—or thirty-year—period in this century." Kennedy, however, never gave that speech. He never left Dallas on that sunny November afternoon.

ASSASSINATION

Around 12:30 p.m., three shots rang out from a building along Kennedy's parade route. One shot hit Kennedy in the throat and then struck Texas Governor John Connally, who was also in the car. Jacqueline scrambled to protect her husband, but there was nothing she could do. The last shot tore through Kennedy's head. Within half an hour, he was dead.

The news spread quickly across the United States and around the world: President Kennedy had been **assassinated**. Stunned Americans wept when they heard the news. The murder of any leader is a terrible shock, but Kennedy was still a young man and he had come to represent a new beginning for the United States.

During his presidency, Kennedy and others had talked about Camelot. In the legend about England's King Arthur, Camelot was the king's castle. Arthur was a strong and popular king with many brave knights who fought for him, and to Kennedy, King Arthur was a hero. Jacqueline Kennedy suggested that the Kennedy White House was like Camelot, with the president as the hero. Now that he was dead, Kennedy seemed an even bigger hero to some Americans. He had lost his life while serving his country.

Lee Harvey Oswald, Kennedy's assassin

AFTER THE ASSASSINATION

Police soon captured John Kennedy's assassin, a man named Lee Harvey Oswald. For a time, Oswald had lived in the Soviet Union, and he also opposed U.S. policies toward Cuba. The nation, though, never learned exactly why Oswald killed the president. Oswald himself was killed two days later while in police custody by Jack Ruby, a Dallas bar owner.

Hours after Kennedy's death, on a plane flying

back to Washington, D.C., Vice President Lyndon Johnson was sworn in as president. Jacqueline Kennedy stood beside him, her suit still stained with her husband's blood. At Kennedy's funeral, the sight of the young widow and her two small children touched many Americans. Three-year-old John Jr. saluting his father's coffin especially moved them.

President Johnson later spoke to Congress about the former president. He said, "Today, John Fitzgerald Kennedy lives on in the immortal words and works that he left behind. He lives on in the mind and memories of mankind. He lives on in the hearts of his countrymen."

Lyndon Johnson being sworn in as president

The Kennedy family mourned the death of JFK.

The Warren Commission

In 1964, President Lyndon Johnson set up a special committee to investigate the murder of John F. Kennedy. Chief Justice Earl Warren (above center) of the U.S. Supreme Court led the investigation. The Warren Commission found that Lee Harvey Oswald acted alone. They said there was no **conspiracy** to kill the president.

Some Americans, however, do not accept this finding and argue even today that there was a conspiracy to kill Kennedy. Many books have been written trying to prove that U.S. government officials or criminals planned the assassination. In 1978, a committee from Congress said a conspiracy could not be completely ruled out.

In 1992, Congress ordered the release of thousands of documents related to Oswald and the assassination. None of the evidence showed that Oswald had help in the assassination of President Kennedy.

REMEMBERING JFK

For a few years, most Americans continued to remember Kennedy as a hero. Over time, however, historians began to uncover information about Kennedy and his family, and Americans learned how Joseph Kennedy had used his power and money to help John's career. People also learned about times when John Kennedy and his brother Bobby lied about their actions. Some critics said Kennedy was not the hero many Americans thought he was—or that Kennedy wanted to be.

opposite: John F. Kennedy will long be remembered.

Brother Bobby

Shortly after John Kennedy's assassination, Bobby Kennedy retired as attorney general. In 1964, he was elected as a U.S. senator from New York. Bobby wanted to continue some of the policies started by his brother, including his work for civil rights. He also backed the war in Vietnam, though later he changed his mind about the U.S. presence there.

In 1968, Bobby decided to run for president. He won support from many young voters and people who had admired John. Like his brother, however, Bobby faced an assassin's bullet. On June 6, 1968, Bobby was shot and killed while campaigning for the Democratic presidential nomination in California. Once again, the country grieved for a prominent young leader named Kennedy.

However, many Americans remember the good things Kennedy did. They recall his actions during the Cuban Missile Crisis, they remember how he tried to help the poor, and they look back on his efforts to improve rights for minorities. Some Americans still weep over Kennedy's brutal death, and others honor his role as the first Roman Catholic president. Many Americans also remember the energy the young president brought to the nation as the champion of a New Frontier.

The Kennedy Clan

Over the years, the Kennedy family has remained famous but has also suffered its share of tragedies. In 1994, Jacqueline Kennedy Onassis died of cancer. Five years later, John F. Kennedy Jr. died in a plane crash on the way to a family wedding, and the nation mourned that loss. Nevertheless, the Kennedys continue to believe in the ideals of public service. John's brother Edward (above center) has been a senator from Massachusetts since 1962, and other Kennedys have served in Congress and local offices.

TIMELINE

1917	John F. Kennedy is born on May 29 in Brookline, Massachusetts
1939	Travels in Europe
1940	Graduates from Harvard University; publishes *Why England Slept*
1941	Enters the U.S. Navy
1943	Captains *PT 109* in the South Pacific Ocean
1946	Wins election as a U.S. representative from Massachusetts
1952	Wins election as a U.S. senator from Massachusetts
1953	Marries Jacqueline Lee Bouvier
1956	Is considered a possible vice presidential candidate for the Democratic Party
1957	Receives Pulitzer Prize for *Profiles in Courage*
1960	Defeats Richard Nixon to become the thirty-fifth president of the United States
1961	Faces possible conflict with the Soviet Union after the building of the Berlin Wall; orders the invasion of Cuba's Bay of Pigs by U.S.-trained Cuban exiles in an unsuccessful attempt to overthrow Cuban leader Fidel Castro
1962	Successfully forces the Soviet Union to remove missiles from Cuba
1963	Is assassinated on November 22 in Dallas, Texas

adrenal glands: two glands located near the kidneys that make a hormone called adrenaline

ally: a country that is associated with and supportive of another

ambassador: a person who serves one nation as a representative in another nation

assassinated: murdered by sudden and secret attack

civil rights: the rights of every citizen

Cold War: a conflict without military action between the United States and the Soviet Union

communism: a system in which the government owns everything

conspiracy: a secret criminal plan agreed upon by several people

democratic governments: systems in which the people choose their leaders

economy: the system a country uses to manage its money and business

electoral vote: the vote made by members of the Electoral College—specially elected representatives from each state

famine: a time of extreme food shortage

impeded: hindered the progress of something or someone

inauguration: a ceremony at which someone is sworn into office

malfunction: to fail to work properly

primaries: elections in which people in a certain area (usually a state) vote for delegates to send to their political party's convention

radioactive: giving off radiation, a potentially dangerous form of energy

Roman Catholic Church: a Christian church that is led by the pope in Rome

Soviet Union: a former nation of fifteen republics—now independent nations—that included Russia and the Ukraine

United Nations: an international organization that promotes peace throughout the world

TO FIND OUT MORE

BOOKS

Clinton, Susan. *The Cuban Missile Crisis.* Chicago: Childrens Press, 1993.

Cole, Michael D. *John F. Kennedy: President of the New Frontier.* Springfield, N.J.: Enslow Publishers, 1996.

Coulter, Laurie. *When John and Caroline Lived in the White House.* New York: Hyperion Press, 2000.

Hampton, Wilborn. *Kennedy Assassinated: The World Mourns: A Reporter's Story.* Cambridge, Mass.: Candlewick Press, 1997.

Netzley, Patricia. *The Assassination of President John F. Kennedy.* New York: New Discovery Books, 1994.

Potts, Steve. *John F. Kennedy: A Photo-illustrated Biography.* Mankato, Minn.: Bridgestone Books, 1996.

Sandak, Cass R. *The Kennedys.* New York: Crestwood House, 1991.

Spies, Karen Bornemann. *John F. Kennedy.* Springfield, N.J.: Enslow Publishers, 1999.

INTERNET SITES

CNN Cold War
http://cnn.com/specials/cold.war
To learn more about the Cold War.

Concrete Curtain–Berlin Wall
http://www.wall-berlin.org/gb/berlin.htm
For information about the wall that separated East and West Berlin.

Cuban Missile Crisis
http://www.nsa.gov/docs/cuba/
For details about the 1962 crisis.

Department of the Navy–Naval Historical Center
http://www.history.navy.mil/faqs/faq60-2.htm
For detailed information about John F. Kennedy's service in the U.S. Navy.

John F. Kennedy–Internet Public Library
http://www.ipl.org/ref/POTUS/jfkennedy.html
For information about Kennedy's years as president.

John F. Kennedy Presidential Library
http://www.cs.umb.edu/jfklibrary/index.htm
For biographical details about JFK.

INDEX

Page numbers in *italics* indicate illustrations.

Addison's disease, 9, 22
African-Americans, 28–29, 37
Alliance for Progress, 29
assassination, 5, 37–39

Bay of Pigs, 31
Berlin, Germany, 31–32, *31*, *32*, 33
Berlin Wall, 32, *32*, 33
Birmingham, Alabama, 37
Boston, Massachusetts, 6
Bouvier, Jacqueline Lee. *See* Kennedy, Jacqueline Bouvier.

Camelot, 38
Castro, Fidel, 30, *30*, 34
Catholic religion. *See* Roman Catholicism.
Choate Academy, 8
civil rights, 28–29, *28*, 37, 42, 43
Cold War, 18
Communism, 17–18, 30, 31
Connally, John, 37
Cuban Missile Crisis, 33–34, 43

Dallas, Texas, 36, *36*
Democratic Party, 10, 18, 20, 21, 22, 23, *23*, 24

Eisenhower, Dwight D., 20, 24
electoral votes, 25

Fitzgerald, John F. "Honey Fitz" (grandfather), 7
France, 12, *12*, 31

Germany, 12, 14
Great Britain, 10–12, 31
"Great Debates," 25, *25*

Harris, Charles, 15
Hitler, Adolf, 10

inauguration, 4, *4*, 26–27
Irish immigrants, 6–7
Italy, 14

Japan, 13, 14, 15
Johnson, Lyndon B., 24, *24*, 39, *39*, 40

Kefauver, Estes, 21
Kennedy, Caroline (daughter), 22, *22*
Kennedy, Edward "Ted" (brother), 43, *43*
Kennedy, Jacqueline Bouvier (wife), 5, 18, *19*, 20, *20*, 22, *22*, 26, *36*, 37, 38, 39, *39*, 43
Kennedy, John Fitzgerald, *4*, *5*, *6*, *7*, *8*, *10*, *14*, *18*, *19*, *22*, *23*, *24*, *25*, *32*, *35*, *36*, *41*, *43*
  assassination of, 5, 37–39
  athleticism of, 8, *9*
  birth of, 7
  childhood of, *6*, 7–8, *7*
  education of, 8, 9, 11
  health of, 8–9, 16, 22
  journalism career, 17
  marriage of, 18, *19*
  military career, 13–15
  religion of, 22–23
Kennedy, John F., Jr. (son), 26, *26*, 39, *39*, 43

Kennedy, Joseph (father), 6, *6*, 7, *7*, *8*, 9, 10, 14, 18, 40
Kennedy, Joseph, Jr. (brother), 8, 9, 16, *16*
Kennedy, Pat (grandfather), 7
Kennedy, Robert "Bobby" (brother), 18, 26, *27*, *39*, 42, *42*, *43*
Kennedy, Rose (mother), 7, *7*
Khrushchev, Nikita, 32, *32*, 33, 34
King, Rev. Martin Luther, Jr., 37, *37*

malaria, 16
McMahon, Pat, 15, 16

New Frontier program, 5, 24, 27, 43
Nixon, Richard M., 24, *24*, 25, *25*
nuclear weapons, 30, 32, 33, 34

Onassis, Aristotle, 20
Oswald, Lee Harvey, 38, *38*

Peace Corps, 29, *29*
Pearl Harbor, Hawaii, 13, *13*
popular vote, 25
primaries, 24
Princeton University, 8
Profiles in Courage (John F. Kennedy), 21
Protestant religion, 23
PT 109, 14, 15, 16
PT boats, 14, 15
Pulitzer Prize, 21

recession, 28
Republican Party, 24
Roman Catholicism, 4, 23, 43
Roosevelt, Franklin Delano, 10
Ruby, Jack, 38

INDEX *(continued)*

Senate Foreign Relations
    Committee, 21
Soviet Union,
    17–18, 21, 30, 33, 34, 38
space exploration, 5, 30
Starkey, Ray Lee, 15
Stevenson, Adlai, 20, 21

Truman, Harry, 17, 18, 23
Turkey, 33, 34

U.S. Navy, 4–5, 13, 14, *14*

Vietnam, 42

Warren Commission, 40, *40*
Warren, Earl, 40, *40*
Why England Slept (John F.
    Kennedy), 11, *11*
World War I, 10
World War II, 4–5, 10, 11–16,
    12, 13

About the Author

As an editor at *Weekly Reader* for six years, **Michael Burgan** created educational material for an interactive online service and wrote about current events. Now a freelance author, Michael has written more than thirty books, primarily for children and young adults. These include biographies of Secretary of State Madeleine Albright, President John Adams, and astronaut John Glenn. His other historical writings include two volumes in the series American Immigration and books on the Declaration of Independence and the Boston Tea Party. Michael has a bachelor of arts degree in history from the University of Connecticut and resides in that state.